S0-BJS-035

31-23

LITURGY
IN
FOCUS

LITURGY
IN
FOCUS

by
GERARD S. SLOYAN

ST. JOSEPH'S UNIVERSITY
BTQ 4143 .S63L   STX
Liturgy in focus,

3 9353 00017 9315

66597

DEUS BOOKS
Paulist Press
(Paulist Fathers)
Glen Rock, N.J.

ACKNOWLEDGMENT

Grateful acknowledgment is made to H. M. Mackin and *Hi-Time Publishing Co.*, Elm Grove, Wisconsin, for generous permission to use the copyrighted material contained in these pages.

NIHIL OBSTAT: Austin B. Vaughan, S.T.D.
Censor Librorum

IMPRIMATUR: ✠ Francis Cardinal Spellman
Archbishop of New York

April 30, 1964

The NIHIL OBSTAT and IMPRIMATUR are official declarations that a book or pamphlet is free of doctrinal or moral error. No implication is contained therein that those who have granted the NIHIL OBSTAT and IMPRIMATUR agree with the contents, opinions or statements expressed.

Copyright © 1964 by
The Missionary Society
of St. Paul the Apostle
in the State of New York

Library of Congress
Catalog Card Number: 64-20244

Cover Design: CLAUDE PONSOT

Published by the Paulist Press
Editorial Office: 304 W. 58th St., N.Y., N.Y. 10019
Business Office: Glen Rock, N. J. 07452

Manufactured in the
United States of America

24

Contents

5

To my sister Elizabeth,
known in the world as
Sr. M. Thomas Aquinas, O.P.

Introduction

If a motion picture is briefly out of focus the audience groans. A badly focused lens will spoil every snapshot taken until it is adjusted. Eye-glasses that are improperly fitted, or that stay the same while the eyes change, can do permanent harm to the eyes.

Any form of sacramental worship that is not in focus threatens the faith and the piety of those who pray by means of it. Sacramental prayer—that is to say, liturgy—which is in focus at a time when the understanding that Christians have of it is not in focus, presents a different kind of threat to faith and piety.

When the Catholics of the world learned on December 4, 1963, from the press, radio, and television that those of their number who prayed in Latin could look forward to radical changes in the forms of all the sacraments including the Mass, many were disturbed. What did the bishops of Vatican Council II under Pope Paul mean by the "Constitution" they voted on so overwhelmingly? Couldn't they leave well enough alone in a sensitive area like that of a Christian believer at his prayer?

7

Then came reports, first in winter, then in spring, that the bishops of the U.S. were going to present proposals to the Holy See for the use of considerable English in the Mass, the other sacraments, and the sacramentals. Many sighed with relief at that. At least nothing much was going to change except the language of some of the familiar prayer forms. The Holy See would give the approval Pope Paul promised when he declared the Constitution to be in force (Feb. 16, 1964), and that would be that. Many priests and parishioners don't read so well publicly, it was thought, but at least one would still be able to get the meaning of the Mass from reading his missal.

This little book is written to try to put in focus the badly blurred notion expressed immediately above. First of all, the rites of our liturgical prayer in the West have gone out of focus over the centuries; that must be corrected, said the Council Fathers, by the diligent work of a post-conciliar Commission which will make them meaningful again. Secondly, the entire Western Church has lost precision on the question of what happens at Mass, at a baptism, at an ordination, or a funeral. Priests and people alike need readjustment. They need to rediscover the community nature of sacramental prayer; to come to learn, perhaps for the first time, the importance of sacred song in worship; to appreciate anew the living Word that is first proclaimed to them in Scripture and sermon, then celebrated in the sacrificial rite that is the supper of the Lord. In brief, the whole Catholic community of the West must improve its focus on celebration in any language before the use of English in celebration can be a boon to it rather than a novelty or annoyance.

These pages are offered to anyone who may be helped by them. They are written simply because the Word of God is simple, as are the Deed done in Christ that saves us, and the forms of celebration that bring us life in virtue of this saving act.

1
Liturgy Means Prayer in Action

LITURGY is not a word you're going to hear on television in your next few nights of viewing —nor in your next few months, one would be safe to say. It sounds like another English word, "lethargy," which is a pretty good synonym for watching TV. The big difference is that lethargy means doing *nothing,* and liturgy means doing *something.*

Our word "lethargy" traces its origin back to the Greek word *lethe.* In Greek mythology, anyone who drank the waters of the river Lethe tended to forget. But we participate in the liturgy to *remember,* not to *forget.* The "lit" in liturgy comes from the Greek word for *people;* the second part of the word is the term for *work.* The liturgy reminds us that the major *work* of God's holy *people* (the Church) is *the praise of God.*

We who belong to the Church wouldn't have a clue on how to praise God best unless His Son had told us. We worship God chiefly, of course, by giving Him our thoughts and our hearts: what the Mass at one point calls "spiritual service." But *the exact form this worship ought to take is where the problem lies.*

The Son of God settled the question for us by becoming God's perfect servant, His minister. The service Christ gave God while on earth was a totally obedient human mind and will; the sign of this obedience was His death on the cross. Holy Mass is simply acting out, in the order of symbol or sign, this perfect work of service (worship, praise) done by Jesus on Calvary and completed in His resurrection-ascension.

The liturgy, above all else, is an *act of Christ*. But He does not do this deed alone. Because we are members of Christ's body—His mystical body the Church—*we,* too, take part in this act of His. If our thoughts and dispositions become Christ's, then each time the liturgy is celebrated we join ourselves with Christ in the worship of God. The one body of Christ—the "whole Christ," as Saint Augustine puts it—does the work of praising God for His great glory.

Liturgy is normally marked by ceremonial— the kind of carefully spelled-out behavior that takes place in a royal court, or when men do anything especially solemn like marrying or burying. Still, the heart of any liturgy is not its music, nor its slow and stately gestures, nor its appeal to the senses.

Liturgy is primarily *prayer in action*—action by a group of people all of whom have the same intention and purpose: the worship of God. Because they are united in the work that needs doing (praise of God in sign), they get together on how to do it. Songwise, posturewise, majestic prayerwise—if you'll forgive the barbarisms—they agree upon a way of praising the Father under the headship of Jesus Christ. It is the Holy Spirit who leads them to this unity of worship; but He can only do so because He has first brought them into one as a holy people—the Church.

"Liturgy," then, is the word to use when you mean the unity of men at prayer—that prayer which is the prayer-in-act of Jesus Christ.

2
Prayer ... Alone and with Others

THERE was a report in *Time* last year about the ugly situation in South Africa called *apartheid*. In Afrikaans (the language of many in South Africa), this word describes the enforced segregation of Negroes and "Cape Coloreds" from whites. At the end of this report appeared an old, old joke—Lou Holtz used to tell it about the Jewish "high holy days"—in which a white policeman enters a South African church on a Sunday and finds a lone black man on his knees. "What are you doing, Kaffir?" (a Bantu tribesman), the policeman asks him. "Scrubbing the floor," the African gentleman says. "Okay," says the officer, "but God help you if I catch you praying!"

Now the basic thing wrong with that joke—if you'll pardon our ruining it by analyzing it—is that it doesn't seem to recognize the difference between *public* and *private* prayer. It fails to distinguish the two by supposing that the white policeman would really mind if he *did* catch the Negro praying. But of course he wouldn't.

Neither would any white member of the community, for that matter. They would, in fact, probably fight for the right of the Negro to pray on his knees in their church—provided he was praying alone. It is only the thought of his praying with *them*, in their church, as part of a group to which both he *and they* belong, that they cannot endure.

This then, is the first thing we must talk about if we're going to be discussing the liturgy in this book: the difference between private and public prayer, prayer alone and prayer in a group.

When a man goes into his room late at night, kneels down beside his bed and tries to lift his thoughts to God, he pleases Him in that he prays. If three or four nights before this he has joined his wife and three small children in their night prayers before the youngsters go to bed, he also will have pleased his Father in heaven. The next morning on his way to work, he climbs out at the corner where his car-pool drops him and stops in at a church before going to his office. The Mass is over and some three hundred people in the church are saying the prayers of a novena. He picks up a card and joins them.

All three of these times the man was engaging in *private prayer*.

Two mornings later he goes to Mass at 6:30 in his parish church before his car-pool picks him up. There are eleven persons in the church, besides the priest and the server. There he takes part in *public prayer*.

What's the difference? Well, chiefly this: "public" has the word *populus* in it, meaning "people." At Mass—alone of the four times the man prayed—he prayed the great prayer of God's holy people. Every time he prayed, he was as much a member of the Church, God's holy people, as when he was at Mass. But only at Mass did he do the great public act of the Church under the headship of Christ. He praised God through the sacrifice of Jesus our Lord in the unity of the Holy Spirit. He took part in the prayer *of* God's people *as* God's people.

A month later he goes to an infant niece's baptism. Six months after that he goes to his grand aunt's home and prays with the priest while she is anointed in her serious illness. A year later he makes a layman's retreat at a monastery and follows along as the monks sing the divine office. At each of these times he prays the public prayer of God's holy people: he takes part in the liturgy.

What about his morning and night prayers, either with his family or alone? Don't they count?

Of course they do.

These prayers not only have value in themselves but also (and chiefly) they prepare him to take his part in the prayer of the Church led by Christ: the Mass, the other sacraments and sacramentals, the divine office, and all the blessings that a bishop gives—for a bishop is Christ acting in the Church in a way no other Christian does.

3
The Liturgy a Bishop Celebrates

I T IS a great occasion when the bishop of your diocese comes to your parish to confirm, or just to pay a pastoral visit. It is a "great day," not only because you don't see him very often, or because he is a V.I.P., but because our bishop is *Christ* to us in a way that no one else is.

One of the famous martyrs of the early Church, Saint Ignatius, Bishop of Antioch in Syria, wrote in a letter just before he died that where a bishop's Eucharist is celebrated, there is the Church. He was saying that the bishop is the visible sign of our unity as God's holy people. The bishop gives us the holy bread which, when we eat it, forms us into the one body of Christ. That is another way of saying that the Church is *one* because the bishop makes it to be so through the *one Eucharist* that he presides over.

The ordinary priest in the Church has a sacred

work to do because he is someone and does something in relation to a bishop. The bishop doesn't ordain him and then say to him, "Now, Father, for the rest of your priesthood you're on your own." You can wind up a mechanical toy that way, but not a man. This is especially true of someone who must be in a close and loving relation with Christ for a lifetime. The Church's way of keeping the priest in touch (she has never had another way) is through his bishop. The priest is a co-worker with his bishop, under his direction.

The book that contains the prayers and ceremonies of sacraments and blessings celebrated by a bishop is called the "Pontifical"—an adjective made from a Latin word for bishop. The ordination rites for the "minor" and "major" orders are there, from the lowest one of "doorkeeper" to the highest one of bishopric, that is, the priesthood in its fullness. When a bishop consecrates an altar, a church, or a chalice, when he celebrates a Mass, his liturgical actions are all spelled out for him in the Pontifical. He is also directed by the Church to have his clergy and people join him actively in the sacred work of celebrating the Christian mysteries.

Our bishops are our leaders in what is called the "modern liturgical revival." They have been hard at work at the Second Vatican Council on the important changes in the structure and language of the liturgy that will bring Christian people closer to the living Christ. They scrutinized their own liturgical celebration as bishops in a special way, both because it is so important (our bishop is the "high priest" in our diocese), and because so many long ceremonies in the Pontifical have lost their meaning for both bishops and people. In the document they framed on the liturgy, which Pope Paul promulgated on December 4, 1963, they proposed a revision of their special rites (like priestly ordination and confirmation), as well as *all* the other rites of the Western liturgy.

When a bishop comes to our parish or when we visit his cathedral (which is everybody's parish church)—let's say, for instance, at the Mass of Chrism on Holy Thursday morning—we should not come out saying: "My, that was impressive. So solemn!" Or "Was that ever *long!*" We should have taken part in something so meaningful and moving that we will say: "I've never understood until today what people mean when they say, '*Christ* acts through the sacraments.'"

4
Holy Mass
the Supreme Liturgy

A NY human being who lives only for compli-
ments is rightly called *vain*. We all like to
hear nice things said about ourselves, but if praise
or flattery becomes food and drink to us, we are
usually in deep trouble on the personality front.

It's the same situation when people wish to be
waited on, hand and foot. Wanting to turn everyone into your personal servant is a sure sign
you've lost your grip on reality.

With God, everything is different. God can't
possibly be vain or proud or domineering. God
is all that really is, and He *has* everything He
creates. No one can set His mind at rest by telling
Him how great He is. What we do is to set *our*
minds at rest by telling Him so.

Actually, the word "worship" means "worth-
ship." At times in the past, the acknowledgment
of God's glory or worth has been called His

*ex*trinsic glory—glory from *outside* Himself. This is the glory which God's creatures—angels and men—give Him. Because they are God's creatures, they need to give God glory; it doesn't just *happen.*

This praise of God doesn't represent any need God has. It is a need that God's creatures have. Unless these creatures praise God for His great glory, they are going to be incomplete as creatures. If they fail to worship God their Creator, the entire balance of the universe will be upset.

You know well what our Christian belief is about the true worship of God. Our faith holds that Jesus Christ, who is God's own Son, gives to His Father perfect praise. Jesus did this throughout His life, but especially in His obedient death. As a reward or response to this perfect obedience of His, the Father raised Him up at His "right hand," where in eternal glory He now offers perfect praise.

This praise which Christ offers is sometimes called the "heavenly liturgy." The New Testament book called the Apocalypse (Revelation) is chiefly concerned with the glory which Jesus— "the Lamb"—gives to God in the heavenly city. Everything is described as though it were taking place in the throne room of the great King. Jesus is the lamp, a bright light shining in that court where "there shall be no night."

The time sequence in the vision of the biblical author is of the past, the present, and the future. The Mass is the enacting of the sacrifice of Calvary where Christ offered Himself in His physical body to His heavenly Father. The Mass is also the present offering by Christ of His mystical body on earth. The Mass points to a fulfillment in heaven where Christ at this moment continues to lead the praise and adoration of the saints and angels in glory.

That means that our Mass is (1) a sign that really represents the past, (2) our acting together with Christ now, and (3) a pledge of our future glory. It is hard for us to grasp with our human minds the timelessness of the Mass.. Saint John, the poet-seer to whom the Apocalypse is attributed, saw the enactment of the *heavenly liturgy*: the praise and adoration given to God by the glorified Lamb of God surrounded by the saints and angels.

We, as saints-in-the-making, share in the *earthly liturgy*. Both are real, but in different ways. Christ's one perfect act of praise, adoration, thanksgiving, and reparation is done in sign for us on earth because of our continuing need of redemption. It is a glorious actuality in heaven where all has been perfectly achieved. Christ pleads for us and sums up the gratitude of the saints in glory. This He can do because He is our head upon earth and the head of the court of heaven.

What a vision this is! And what a reality!

5
Sacraments Other Than the Eucharistic Sacrifice

G OD has told us that He is essentially LOVE. This is the mystery of His being. In one sense He is unapproachable but in another sense He is very close to us. He wishes to take us to Himself and to give us His life in its fullest measure.

The way God has chosen to approach us is through His Son, Jesus—and Jesus is also our way back to Him. It is in Jesus that God has communicated His love and shared His life. So the mystery of God (the mystery of love, remember) is the mystery of Christ.

Now, at the center of the mystery of Christ is the Easter mystery. This is the fact—retained by the Church as a memory—of the glorious return of Jesus, in the Spirit, to His Father after His obedient life which ended in His bloody death in the flesh.

This event took place at one point in *history*.

Now it is extended through time in *mystery*. In other words, we come into possession of that life which Christ promised us by celebrating the Mass ("the mystery of faith," a consecration prayer calls it), in a spirit of faith.

There is a postcommunion prayer in the missal (for Wednesday of Holy Week) that speaks of this very beautifully: "Deepen our capacity, O almighty God, trustingly to believe that by Your Son's death in time, which these holy mysteries represent, You have granted us life in eternity." The "holy mysteries," of course, are the eucharistic action itself: God's love for us, expressed in terms of the passion, resurrection, and ascension of Christ, made present in sacrament (*i.e.*, sign).

Making present this love God has for us in His Son is the heart of the liturgy. We might put it another way by saying that the Mass is the high point of that sign language which we speak to God and God speaks to us. But while the Mass is the high point, it is not the only point. There is more speaking, more exchange. There are many other signs that bring the life of God to us. Six of them, the other six sacraments, are special among these signs in that they stand for and thus convey God's life in a way that other signs (*viz.*, sacramentals and indeed all creatures) do not.

They are not on a par with the Eucharist, because while they transmit the life, hence love, of God (or grace, as it's often called), only the Eucharist contains the God of love Himself. Baptism brings us to birth; it establishes the love-relation of sonship. Confirmation is the special gift of the Spirit in which He comes to us "in His fullness" to make us more like Christ. Penance restores the love-relation if we have destroyed it through sin. Holy orders are designed to raise up deacons, priests, and bishops, men who will continue the signs that make the Church a community of love. Marriage raises up new lovers of God and believers in Christ; a man's love for his wife also reminds us how much Christ loves His Church. The anointing of the sick ("extreme unction" in archaic speech) prepares us for glory, if we are old or in God's plan fall seriously ill and may die.

Let's do it another way. Baptism and confirmation give us the power to offer Christ to God and eat Him as our food through giving us a share in His priestly power. Penance removes any barrier that would keep us from the feast. Marriage populates the holy table with family members who love. Holy orders provide us with the men who can set and serve the banquet. The last anointing restores us in good health to the Church around the altar, or else readies us for our final Eucharist.

At the center of this little "universe" of signs is the "sun," the body and blood of Christ, the Eucharist. It is the great sign of the mystery of God's love. The lesser signs, the other sacraments, like planets, derive all their power and light from it. The sacramentals—chiefly blessings, but also bits of sacred behavior and objects that have been rendered sacred through blessings —derive all their force from the sacraments.

6
The Divine
Office

AN OFFICE is the place where the school principal is. It is also a room filled with people busy transcribing shorthand onto eight-and-a-half by eleven-inch paper by typewriter. We use the word "office" in other ways, too. We read that so-and-so ran for public office. Or the governor's best friend may say, "The governor is looking older. He is worn by the cares of office."

Here, "office" means *duty* or *obligation*: what you have to do. When we are speaking of people in love, we normally don't refer to the duty they have of loving one another. "Muriel just got a ring from Frank. Poor thing, she's obliged to love him now." That isn't the way Muriel thinks. She's crazy-mad to do anything Frank asks because she loves him so much. But love grows tired as the years pass. It can become forgetful. Love needs to be reminded of its duties. There

24

are certain obligations that come with saying, "I am in love."

In the Church, priests have a high privilege and a great responsibility. So, too, do "religious" —monks and nuns in monasteries, and religious priests and sisters and brothers. All these Christians take on definite obligations as part of their way of expressing love for God and others in Jesus Christ.

Aside from not marrying and living obedient and plain lives (some even poor), many religious pray the "divine office" every day. They take on a godly obligation, in other words. This duty is sometimes called the "work of God." It is prayer said or sung for all who are too busy earning a living to take on any such daily burden.

This "office" is the prayer of the *whole* Church. It is part of the liturgy. In the strict sense, it is public prayer—the people's prayer. The divine office is composed of readings from the Bible, chiefly the singing or saying of the one hundred and fifty sacred poems in the Old Testament known as psalms.

Bible reading followed by solid thinking about what the holy books mean is as old as the Church herself. Something like this is done whenever the epistle and the gospel are read at Mass. At the baptism of a new Christian or the anointing of a sick person prayers are said. If the person is an adult and conscious of what's going on, nothing prepares him better to receive the sacred sign that gives him God's grace than hearing the Holy Scriptures read prayerfully.

All day long the Church is chanting or reading the divine office somewhere. Its prayers are both the perfect preparation for the Mass of that day and the perfect follow-up of that Mass. When you see a priest reading his "breviary," you know that he is continuing the Church's Mass liturgy for that day. He is reading psalms and other Scripture and also man-made prayers. These serve the Mass as a setting serves a precious stone.

Any Christian can pray the divine office — every day if he wishes. There are one-volume, short forms in English done by several different publishers. The entire office in its present form is available in English and Latin in three volumes from one publisher, and in one volume in English from another.

How would you like to make up "your own divine office" for one day?

It's easy. Just copy the day's collect out of your missal. Find its main idea. Then look up in your Bible a psalm (or two or three) that seems to carry out this idea. Punctuate your day with these psalms and this prayer. You'll be joining in with a chorus of thousands who are doing the same thing.

Jesus Christ is the great Leader in this prayer. He is the Choirmaster in this song of praise to the Father that the Church prays every day.

7
Blessings
of the Church

GOD means "holiness itself." Everything He has made has a certain share in the holiness He Himself is. Yet there is another way for persons and things to share in the holiness of God besides being created by Him. It is by giving oneself over to Him, or dedicating objects to Him in a special way.

The word "sacred" is hidden somewhere in the middle of the word "consecrate." The sacredness of God (His holiness or "Godness") is passed on to a statue carved from stone, or to a silver cup, or to a man or woman, when the object or person is set aside for a special purpose. We really have only one big purpose in life: to praise God through Jesus Christ in the Spirit. This praise is our liturgy.

All the people and all the objects employed in the work of praise need to have something of the

sacredness of God about them if they are to do
the job well. They acquire this holiness (yes,
even pieces of marble or wood acquire it) by
being blessed by a holy sign performed by a holy
man. You understand, of course, that all creatures have a kind of headstart on sacredness
through being made by a holy God.

It is growing clearer, isn't it, that "holiness"
or "blessedness" is something that results from
closeness to God. When a father at home makes
the sign of the cross on his children's foreheads at
night, when the Church consecrates a virgin or
receives the religious vows of a brother-candidate,
when a bishop ordains a man to the priesthood,
all who are blessed are expected to *act* holier.
Basically this is because they *are* holier, whether
they ever perform a single act or not. It is near-
ness to God that makes a person sacred or an
object blessed.

The Church's greatest blessing or consecration
is the Mass. There, ordinary food (bread and
wine) becomes holy by being changed into the
living Jesus Christ and being offered to God
the All-Holy. God accepts the gift that is made
to Him in symbol of His Son; this makes the eucharistic gifts, already holy through being set
aside for the purpose, holier still. Become the full
reality of His Son, they are now wholly God's,
and He gives them back to us to eat. This means
that the Eucharist is sacred food in three ways:
(1) God made it; (2) it is now the body, blood,
and soul of His Son, and His divinity; and (3)
God has accepted this offering made to Him by

Christ and the Church. The Eucharist becomes God's special possession, and He makes of it our food.

Now that we have the idea of the Church's *chief* blessing, it should be easy to understand her lesser ones. Every time this holy family ("God's people") does something by way of words and gestures to set a thing apart for His service, she makes it especially His. She "charges" it with the holiness of God.

All through the Mass there are blessings of the people, of incense, of the food and drink as it is being readied. Each one of the sacraments is accompanied by many blessings (over water, over oil, over salt, both before they are used and during their use). Rosaries are blessed; so are medals and palms and ashes. Why? To charge the air with sacredness, as it were, so that when we come to the sacred conversation that is prayer, in the great consecrations, we will be ready for it. We get ready for the *sacraments* with *sacramentals*.

The priest's Mass book (Missal) contains many blessings. We can find others in a book known as the Roman Ritual and in a collection of prayers that contain indulgences called the *Raccolta* (Italian for "harvest").

See how the Church brings creation into church, as it were, or better, brings God's creation before Him. The Church shows us how to praise God through a person or a thing that is a mute kind of prayer just by existing *as* blessed.

8
Pious Exercises and the Liturgy

D O YOU say the rosary every day in October?
Have you ever taken part in a Corpus Christi procession? In Ireland the Catholics have one favorite litany, in the Ukraine still another. There can easily be a third country where the Catholics do not have a favorite litany at all but are fine Catholics nonetheless.

All the things we have been mentioning are matters of choice in the Church. Some Catholics do not know about the devotion known as the way of the cross; others do not use prayer beads extensively. However, all Catholics have holy Mass and the other six sacraments, and the prayer of the Church (the "divine office"), and the blessings of persons and things.

These three, necessary for the life of the whole Church, are the Church's public prayer, her liturgy. The other things mentioned are not her prayer as a whole Church but are things various groups of Christians do to prepare themselves for offering the prayer of the whole Church. They are less important than the liturgy. Yet, if we did not have them, who can say whether we would be ready to celebrate the liturgy fittingly?

Looking to the title of this chapter, we see that *piety* has to do with the respect, the considerateness, indeed the awe, that should mark our relations with those above us. Piety can be infused into any deed or act. Consequently when a filled church rings out with an English hymn at evening devotions, the people there are participating in what the Church calls a *pious exercise*. It is not the liturgy proper but it is somewhat related to it. This is not nearly as good, obviously, as taking part in the liturgy. Singing the *Gloria* in Latin or English as part of the Mass is, just as obviously, a higher form of prayer than the pious exercise.

Some exercises of piety are not closely related to the liturgy at all—for example, a novena to an obscure saint or prayers that concentrate exclusively on requests for favors.

If all (both liturgy and exercise) are prayers said in a spirit of faith, what is the difference? Just this: the liturgy is a work of the Church under the headship of Christ the redeemer. It is always connected with the central fact: that Christ died, rose, and ascended to His Father (the single saving or redeeming action done by God). We cannot fully understand this mystery of Christ, but we can pray it, celebrate it, and come to love it.

In a pious exercise the human wills of all those who happen to say this prayer, or are familiar with this devotion, are united in a general way. But it isn't a work of the whole Church everywhere.

It can also happen that such an act of piety is rather badly separated or "divorced" from the central mystery of our redemption. Like a seed that goes astray on the wind, it becomes the kind of plant that it is by a necessity of nature, but it may become a wild weed or a solitary bloom that has nothing in common with the rest of the garden.

The best of pious exercises, the Church says, are those that bear a *close* relation to the divine liturgy.

9
The Liturgy
and Song

I T ALL began with a letter about music in church. What did? Why the keen interest of our time in the participation of the faithful in the liturgy, the Church's public prayer.

Pope Saint Pius X, in 1903, wrote to all the bishops of the Western Church everywhere, expecting them in turn to get the word to their people about sacred song as a way to "awaken the Church in the soul." His letter took its name from its first words in Italian, *Tra le sollecitudini* ("Among the cares . . .").

It is called a *motu proprio*. That means that the Pope had the idea himself; no one prompted him, nor was he settling a difficulty that someone else had proposed. This letter, written in the first year Saint Pius was pope, began that reawakening in the West of what the Church is and how she worships God in sacramental celebration. The reawakening is known as the *liturgical renewal*.

Letters usually require an answer. The Holy Father got one in some parts of the world but not in others. Whole dioceses and parishes and religious houses of the Western rites (those that use Latin) began to sing again the music known as plain chant (or plain song). It is often called Gregorian chant for Pope Saint Gregory the Great, chief figure (around 600 A.D.) in the formation of the Roman rite.

The Western bishops also revived the excellent hymns, ancient and modern, written in the same spirit as the chant by men like Giovanni da Palestrina and Orlando di Lasso. One difficulty was that the Pope asked that everything sung as part of the liturgy be sung in Latin. That is understandable, or at least it was sixty-some years ago. It *is* a Latin liturgy, after all, in its foundations, and forever will have been one no matter what language we come to pray it in.

The drawback was that trained choirs took over while the people in the churches sat there, as much "mute spectators" as ever before. Or else the people ground out bad plain chant in a kind of musical doggerel. If you know the Requiem Mass introit or *Credo III* in a version, that really swings, you'll recognize the phenomenon. This was the very opposite of what the Pope had intended by his letter. There were a few exceptions. *Credos I* and *III* got to be pretty well known, and the *Missa de Angelis* (basically not very good music, but catchy) achieved some popularity. So did the Mass for the dead. All of them, especially the latter, were being sung in a jerky sort of rhythm quite unlike the flow of Gregorian chant because the modern, measured music that people are used to is so different.

To help achieve what all the twentieth-century popes have asked for, namely sung prayer at the celebration of the liturgy (actually they asked for it *in* the liturgy, but failure to solve the language problem rendered this impossible), the bishops and other leaders gradually made the *Low Mass with song* the more usual thing. This did not happen in monasteries, where everyone knew Latin. But in the crowded churches of city and country, where practically no one can pronounce Latin (much less think in it), more hymns were being sung that spoke the themes of the Mass.

A sacred hootenanny is an awful thing: twangy tunes from nineteenth-century operettas, like "Mother At Your Feet Is Kneeling" (a Civil War tearjerker entitled "Just Before The Battle Mother"), etc. The Church dislikes that sort of thing because it cheapens what is sacred. What she loves is good poetry that describes the action of the liturgy, set to moving music. What she will love better but hasn't got yet in the West is popular music in the people's language that *is* liturgy.

Does good hymnody, in the liturgical spirit, exist? Look into *Our Parish Hymnal, The Parish Mass Book, Our Parish Prays and Sings, The Pius X Hymnal, The New Saint Basil's Hymnal, The Christian Hymnal.*

Pray for the mammoth work, of composing choral liturgies, after the reform of rites, in the music and language of all the earth.

10
The Five Senses
in the Worship of God

MAYBE you know that old story of a craftsman in stone who was working on a cathedral who spent month after month on a carved figure to be placed so high up that no one would see it. "That's all right," he said quietly, his eye cocked toward unborn generations, "God will see it."

God saw his painstaking labor and must have been pleased about *that,* but as to gazing at a carved figure for eons, our heavenly Father couldn't care less. Sculpture is meant to glorify God, of course. So are fine architecture and good glass and sweet-smelling incense and melodious song. We don't make works of art and bury them in church cellars or sing our best songs down an empty mineshaft.

We create and compose them to delight each other, for *we* are the ones who need our spirits conditioned for prayer, engaged in prayer. All these can help us to pray better, to glorify God by our thoughts and our words, spoken or sung.

Angels don't need handsome sanctuaries, or baptisteries that are symphonies of color. They have lots of sense, but they haven't any senses. We are different. There is no way to our thoughts but through the five senses. If a man were born never seeing, hearing, tasting, touching, or smelling, he would know absolutely nothing. All the roads to his inner self would have been blocked.

When a person lives mostly for sense pleasure he is badly confused about life. The glutton, the curious one who has to experience every sight and touch sensation, the stereo or jazz addict who is nearly driven mad by silence—all these persons abuse the delicate balance between sense and spirit. Here the error is excess: "too much."

There can also be an error by defect: "not enough." We can declare that since God wishes to be worshiped in spirit and in truth He is displeased when we make our churches beautiful, or acoustically correct for organ and human voice. The Manichean and Puritan traditions in Christianity have declared this.

Some Protestant churches have said the same in the past. They feared the senses as potential avenues of evil. They thought that pure worship would be corrupted by the temptation to stop at sense satisfaction, never moving on to actual prayer. The reformers who were "evangelicals" (that is, interested in the Scriptures as the sole rule of faith) had their reasons. They had seen too many artists paint their mistresses and call the picture a Madonna, and too many popes and princes turn churches into museums in the hope that they would be remembered as patrons of the arts.

The Catholic and Orthodox principle—which most Protestants of today subscribe to thoroughly —is quite different from either extreme. It is solidly in between.

We give to God the best that we are capable of in the arts, provided what we produce is sacred in intention and hence qualified for God and His service. But we do not give it to Him directly. We give the joys of sense *to each other*. That helps all of us to give God our hearts.

11
Sanctifying
Sunday

A COMMUNIST newspaper in Cuba lately carried a long and serious article by a young revolutionary journalist. He was scolding the Cuban people for continuing to keep *bourgeois* (*i.e.*, middle class) holidays, as he called them, chiefly the Sunday. While he didn't mention specific types of time-wasting behavior, participating in holy Mass would come first on his list. He contented himself with naming some ways to spend the day well. His chief concerns were hard work for the cause of the revolution, increasing economic productivity, and the like. Then in the quieter parts of the day, he said, one could study the writings of Lenin, Marx, and Engels, and keep up with the great developments that are going on in Cuba.

Both parts of his formula are familiar to Christians—action and leisure—but the Christian employs the formula on different and better terms.

The chief thing we *do* on the Lord's day is perform an action. The mystery of our redemption is presented in sign: we offer Christ to God through sacred symbols (prayer and song, gesture, bread and wine); it is His sacrifice, done by the Church. Then we eat a sacred meal in which Christ's victim body now in glory is the nourishing food. We prepare for this action by having read and explained to us our holy writings, chiefly the Gospel.

Old Israel primarily did *nothing* on the Sabbath. These holy people praised the Lord through their rest, their leisure, while the heathen world around them went about the business of everyday.

The Christians made a change and primarily did *something*, namely, took part in the holy action mentioned above, the eucharistic sacrifice-meal. The Church has none but Jewish ancestry, of course; its early members were well aware of a break in the week's rhythm on a day sacred to the Lord. At first they went about their regular business on Sunday except for Mass (before dawn or at nightfall), both because it wasn't a holiday in the Roman empire and to show their difference from those who kept the Law of Moses and the Sabbath (Saturday). By the time the persecution of the Church had stopped in the early fourth century, and Christianity began to be recognized as the state religion, the Mass-plus-rest principle had been pretty well established. It has been that way ever since.

God was the Holy One to the men of the Old Testament. He is our Holy One, too. We know much more about His holiness, in fact, through Christ and in the Spirit. It is very important to us to have a day each week to praise His holiness, a miniature Easter-Pentecost on which to recall all He has done to save us. Sunday is our great feast in the Church. Feasts of our Lady and the Apostles cannot compare with it in importance. Even feasts of our Lord Himself—like those of the Holy Cross and the Transfiguration—are but ways to remind us of the celebration we take part in every Sunday.

Within the last six or eight years there have been some changes, all of them improvements, in the calendar of the Roman Church. They were made as part of the restoration of the importance of Sunday (now ordered by the "Constitution" or decree of Vatican II). Our Church, through her laws and suggestions, is doing her part to remind us of what things are most important. The next step will be a thoroughgoing renewal of our Church calendar and our rite. Right now it is our turn—bishops, priests, and people alike—to make our celebration of the Sunday so inspiring that we will all come out of church "walking on air," having met the Lord as the Word of truth and the Word of life.

12
Feasts
of the Church

THE pattern of Christian life, we said in the last
chapter, is like the routine of life in ancient
Israel. One day out of seven is sacred unto the
Lord. No week goes by that is not sanctified by
the day at the beginning of that week, "the Lord's
Day," Sunday.

Since the work of our redemption (accomplished through Christ's passion, resurrection,
and ascension) is celebrated fifty-two times each
year, the whole year is sanctified by this one
weekly, holy day.

An ordinary year is made up not only of days
and weeks, of course; it is also composed of seasons. A season is a span of several months or
weeks marked by changes in the weather. These
are brought about by the changing position of
the earth with respect to the sun.

In our part of the world there are four seasons.
Many regions have simply two, the wet and the

dry. The major difference in some places (like
the Arctic Circle) may be the amount of light
or darkness. In any case, while it is the phases
of the moon that are responsible for marking
weeks, it is the earth's relation to the sun that
determines the seasons.

In early times the Roman Christians used to
call our Lord the "Sun of Holiness" because He
was central to the universe. It shouldn't surprise
us, therefore, that there are seasons in the Christian year, just as there are seasons in the calendar
year. The celebration of the mysteries of Christ
by which we are saved is done in a cycle or
rhythm, just as spring, summer, autumn and
winter follow one another in a yearly cycle.

The sun doesn't change position but our globe
does. In the same way, Christ the Savior doesn't
change—He is in glory forever at His Father's
right hand—but our need for Him changes, and
our realization of all that He has done for us
changes as well.

In the early years of the Church there was one
great feast only, the paschal feast. One Saturday
night and Sunday morning each spring, Christians brought to mind that great night when Light
conquered darkness and Christ came forth from
the tomb. There was no Holy Thursday or Good
Friday observance for the first three hundred
years of the Church's life. Christ's death, His
rising from the dead, and His return to His
Father, were all remembered on the one feast
of Easter. Then, seven weeks later, this paschal
joy was brought to completion by a celebration

of the Holy Spirit's descent on the Church. There was still but one feast in the Church, we may say: the paschal feast of Easter-Pentecost.

Then gradually our Lord's manifestation to the pagan world began to be celebrated. This was a wintertime feast, established to keep the thoughts of Christians on their Lord and not on the wild, pagan celebration of the shortest days of the year that would soon grow longer. This new Christian feast commemorated the Lord's "showing forth" (*"epiphaneia"* in Greek) to the Magi from the East, His appearance to His own Jewish people at His baptism in the Jordan, and His first miracle at Cana. All these manifestations of Jesus were summed up and celebrated in the winter feast that came to be the Epiphany.

At just about the same time, a particular day was chosen in the West—Rome in fact—to be celebrated as Christ's birthday. December 25 became the day of "Christ's Mass," as it was later to be called in English speech.

That threefold division of manifestation, death and glorification, and promulgation of the Christ-mystery gives us three major seasons in the Church's year: first, Advent, in preparation for Christ's final coming, and His appearance before the world in the flesh in token of His final coming; then Lent, which culminates in the paschal mystery; and finally the further division of the paschal or Easter time known as the Pentecost season, *i.e.*, weeks upon weeks of ordinary life in the Church, that holy community in which the Spirit dwells.

13
The Major Cycles of the Church's Year

TOPSY was the little girl in *Uncle Tom's Cabin* who wasn't quite sure about who her parents were or where she was born. Her answer to all such questions was: "I jes' growed."

The Church's year is something like that: it just "growed." It wasn't planned out, step by step. Christians began simply by celebrating the "Memory of the Lord." Mass was then, as it is now, the "memorial" of the death *and* glorification of Christ. This is why (1) Sunday, the day of the resurrection, was chosen as the weekly day on which to celebrate the holy Eucharist, and (2) *Easter* was the first feast to be specially observed in the Church.

Since it was so important as the feast of the redemption, Christians extended the Easter observance several weeks. *Pentecost* (when the Holy Spirit was poured out upon the young

Church) was considered the completion of the work of redemption. In the fourth century, Christians began to commemorate the holy *"triduum,"* the three days of Christ's death (Friday), His rest in the tomb (Saturday, the day of vigil), and His resurrection (Sunday). It was even earlier than this that the custom had arisen of preparing for the Easter Vigil: Christians fasted and future Christians were instructed in the faith before being baptized at the Vigil. This preparation we now call *Lent*.

One of the two major cycles of the Church's year comprises Lent, Easter, Pentecost. The other lesser cycle is the Christmas-Epiphany cycle. We have mentioned that the Christmas feast began to be celebrated in the fourth century. Following the custom of the day Christians observed a feast of their ruler, Christ the *Kyrios* or Lord. They chose December 25 for its symbolic recall value. It had been a pagan feast in honor of the sun, and Christians wanted to identify Christ as *the* Sun, the Light of the World. In somewhat the same way the feast of the Epiphany arose in the Eastern Church: a feast of the "showing forth" of the Lord.

The custom of preparing for Christmas (parallel to Lent in preparation for Easter) began in Spain and Gaul (modern France) in the fifth century; and just as in the case of Easter which had six weeks of follow-up, so the Christmas-Epiphany cycle continued for several Sundays.

The Church's year wasn't like Topsy in everything, though. It had certain reasons for its growth

What we want to catch hold of especially beyond a rough idea of the historical development, is the *spirit* of the Church's year. That spirit is the spirit of God's work, redeeming us in Christ. Pope Pius XII said that "the liturgical year is no cold and lifeless representation of past events, no mere historical record. Rather, it is Christ Himself, living on in His Church, and still pursuing that path of boundless mercy which, 'going about and doing good,' He began to tread during His life on earth. This He does in order to bring the souls of men into contact with His mysteries, and so make them *live* by them. These *mysteries are now constantly present and active* . . . each of them is, according to its nature and in its own way, the cause of our salvation."

The Church's year is really only one cycle: that of Christ. There is a certain artificiality to dividing it into two or three parts. Each Mass continues the whole work of our redemption, although each mystery and feast brings its special grace through a special emphasis. These mysteries and feasts are not just celebrations of an abstract idea or fact of Christian doctrine but an event: the carrying on of the work of our redemption.

What's important in all this for us? To remember that God wants to share His own life with us through His Son. That Son of His became man, died, and rose in order that we might have life and have it in abundance. Christ wants us to "die to sin and live for Him." The Church's year is a *school of holiness* with Christ present and active in our midst. As our loving teacher

He unites us to the various mysteries of His redemptive word and life and action.

Someday, we'll be asking ourselves: "What *did* happen in 1962?" Vatican II? Relaxation of the cold war? Met the one and only? Learned about life? Lost someone I loved very much?

Lived Christ's life?

14

Preparation:
Vigil, Prayer, Fasting

THERE is a Negro spiritual called "I Ain't a-Goin' to Grieve My Lord No More" in which these lines occur:

> Now some dark night, about twelve o'clock
> This here ol' world's a goin' to reel and rock.

The song refers to the ancient Christian idea that when our Lord Jesus returns in glory He will come in the middle of the night. We can trace this idea back to Christ's own parable of the foolish virgins at the wedding feast, in which He says that the bridegroom will appear at midnight. (Matthew 25:6)

Since the time of the Apostles the idea has existed in the Church that the Lord's second coming would take place during the night, most likely the paschal night (that is, the Saturday before Easter Sunday). After all, ancient Israel had been set free from her slavery in Egypt at night. When Christ the Light came forth from the tomb, He overcame the blackness of night. Why should not His final victory at the end of the world be a conquest of darkness at its deepest or mid-point: midnight?

For these reasons, the notion of a vigil or nightwatch service is well established in the Church. The paschal vigil is the oldest, but there is also midnight Mass on Christmas or its Octave Day (January 1), before a Holy Year (like 1950), or before a Council (like October 11 of 1962). These nights of prayer are not just a novelty designed to keep us up late. In fact Mass at midnight, when it happens, is more the solemn conclusion and summing up of the night prayer service.

Perhaps you have heard of nocturnal adoration societies? Their purpose is not (or should not be) to get fathers and brothers up at 3 a.m. to do a "hard thing," but to prepare them for a great feast-day Mass that is to follow.

Nowadays, vigils are celebrated by the Church over the entire day before a feast. Usually this is done by the celebration of a vigil Mass, the prayers of which are all about *doing penance*. The priest will wear violet vestments, a sign of penance. Fasting is another part of keeping a day of vigil. Christian adults whose health won't suffer are invited to cut down on their eating on the vigil of a feast day. It is the Church's idea that there must be a little "dying to self" so that we can live more to Christ.

Christmas Eve is a day such as that, though now because of so many family celebrations on the 24th we may keep the vigil on December 23. In the United States we fast on December 7 because the 8th is the national patronal feast, Mary's Immaculate Conception. Most Western Catholics keep a vigil, through prayer and fasting, on the day before Mary's Assumption instead. That feast occurs on August 15.

All these practices are just so many ways of trying to make us get our hearts ready for the Christian celebration that will follow. Centuries ago the prophets said to ancient Israel in the Lord's name: "Rend your hearts, and not your garments." It is still very good advice.

Lent, Advent, the ember days, the vigils all make sense if we are looking deeply inside ourselves to examine our readiness of heart. We must be prepared to meet Christ the bridegroom at all times. Every feast, indeed every Sunday and every daily Mass, is a union of our lives with Christ's who will one day come to us finally and forever.

15

The Word of God in the Liturgy

THERE are two great sacraments or signs that we use in the worship of God: the sacrament of the Word, which is Holy Scripture, and the sacrament of the Deed, the acts of Christ made present to us in sacred symbol. Neither is more important to us than the other: both must work together if God is to speak to us and we are to speak to Him in return.

The whole created world is a "word" spoken by God to us. The night sky, a high wind, green growing things: all are lips and a tongue by which He says to us, "I am."

He says special things through special signs, as well. The mighty sea and the rolling rivers say, "I can drown and I can save; I can cleanse and I can sustain life." Oil from the olive tree says, "I can soothe and heal; I can make supple and strong." The bread loaf says, "I keep life

in men. They lean on me; they call me 'staff'."
The wine of the grape says, "I cheer man's heart
and give him joy." Even salt speaks up from
the table to say, "I make food palatable; I always
have and always will; long before refrigeration,
I kept food from spoiling. Men owe me life."

Fire has a message for us. So does wax. So
does the sweet herb, balsam, that can fill a room
with its fragrance.

These are the great signs from the world of
nature that God uses as a "tongue" to address
us. They are common, everyday things—at least
in most parts of the world it is so. The Lord
God wants to be in touch with *all men* through
His Son and His Holy Spirit, and so He uses a
language that *most* men speak. Not all men, of
course; still, the Eskimo and other cultural primi-
tives certainly know water and fire, if not wheat
and grape and olive.

There is one "risk" so to say, that God runs
in all this use of symbols to speak to us. Because
you and I live in a world of tinned and bottled
products, of electric power and jet-stream en-
gines, nature tends to lose its voice for us. How
then shall God make us holy like Himself—make
us Christian—through the universal language of
sign? The danger is that we will no longer have
understood the tongue.

His answer to this is that He speaks to us
always through sacred books that are an encyclo-
pedia of signs, namely the books of the Bible. The
Church never celebrates the mystery of Christ in
the language of symbol without first reading to

us from our holy books. These Scriptures supply clear and accurate meaning to a language that otherwise might be a great puzzle to us. The Old and New Testaments both are announced in our hearing so that we will know how God saved Israel from a drowning, and how He saves us by the waters of baptism; how He fed the Israelites with manna, and how Jesus fed the disciples with fish and a honeycomb after the resurrection; how He, the eternal Father, feeds us with the body of His Son.

If we were to use the signs of the sacraments without understanding their full meaning, they could soon stop bringing us the inner reality of His transforming love. This would lead to superstition and magic. The Church guards against that constantly. She never breaks the bread of the Eucharist with us without first "breaking the bread of the Word" in the epistle, gospel, and sermon. In general, she shares with us the light of understanding which only the Bible can bring, so that there will be no dark places of misunderstanding whatever in our use of sacred signs.

16

The Psalms
in the Liturgy

THE psalms are sacred poems that were written
to be sung. Their earliest setting was the
court of the kings of Juda and later the splendid
Temple built by King Solomon in Jerusalem. The
collection of psalms grew and grew over many
years until it reached the number one hundred
and fifty.

King David is the person whose name is most
closely connected with the writing of the psalms.
Taken all together these songs are called the
"Psalter."

In the last chapter we pointed out how God
speaks a word to us in Holy Scripture which is
meant to give us the meaning of the sign language ("symbolism") spoken by the sacraments
and sacramentals. There is never a time when
the liturgy is celebrated apart from a reading of
God's word to us in the Bible. It is just unthink-

able that there could be any action of Christ through the sacraments without His first speaking to us from the "sacred page" of Scripture.

Central to the Bible are the four gospels. The Lord Jesus lives in the writings of Matthew, Mark, Luke and John in a way He does in no other place. All of the books of Moses (the Law), the writings of the prophets (such as Isaia and Jeremia), and the writings of the sages or wise men (like the author of Job and Ben Sira) are preparations for the fullness of time which comes with Jesus. That is why at Mass on a day like the Ember Saturday we often read a passage, or even a number of passages, from the Old Testament before we read the gospel. It is much more usual, however, to have as our "lesson" (a word meaning something "read out") a portion of a letter of Paul or some other apostle —Peter, James, John, Jude.

The usual order, then, is a message from the Old Testament and/or a New Testament reading, brought to completion by reading the gospel of Jesus Christ. The latter shows how in Jesus all the hopes and longings expressed in the Old Testament are fulfilled.

The oldest and surest way to express thanks for God's spoken word chanted or read aloud is to respond or sing in return. You know what songs Christians like to burst into: the ones they should know best and love best, the psalms. Sometimes nothing will do but a happy shout like *Alleluia!* a word which means "The Lord be praised!" But snatches from the psalms are the usual way to respond to a reading from the Bible, both at Mass and in the other sacraments.

Look in your missal and see where else we sing portions of the psalms. The entrance hymn (introit) is made up of the verses of a psalm; so is the hymn beginning the preparation of the gifts (offertory verse), and also the hymn to be sung while the people are receiving the Lord's body (communion verse). In the Roman missal these psalms are all cut down to a verse or two, but of course the right thing to do—and many parishes do it—is to sing the *whole* song.

Ask your priest to show you his "office book" and point out to you how much the Church's daily prayer is made up of the Psalter. Then, since it's your Christian prayer book as well as his, ask him for some guidance in praying or studying the psalms.

17
The Liturgy's
Man-Made Prayers

MOST of the Catholics we happen to know pray the Roman liturgy. By no means all however. Some are much more familiar with the rite ("form," "observance") of the Order of Preachers ("Dominicans"), or that of the Carmelites. In the cities of Lyons, Milan, and Seville, the Mass structure is slightly different from that in Rome. Many Catholics have never offered a Roman rite Mass. The largest number of these would be the Oriental (or Eastern) Christians who offer Mass in any of eight different rites.

Probably the largest group is composed of those who use the Byzantine (Bi-zan-tin) Rite of Saint John Chrysostom, among them the Ukrainians, Ruthenians, some Hungarians, and the Russians. Other rites in the Catholic Church are the Armenian, Chaldean, Coptic, Ethiopic, Malabar

Maronite, and Syrian (the "Rite of Saint James"). If we seem to have left some people out it's because they use one of the rites listed above though they employ another language. For example, Rumanians, Melkites, Greeks, and Italo-Greeks all use the Byzantine rite.

The point to be made is that there is and always has been in the Church great freedom to make up the prayer forms which Christian men will use. This freedom has certain limits, of course, but we need to realize that the result of this liberty of action has been a great richness in the liturgy of the Church.

Certain things never change, for example the use of bread and wine to become Christ's body and blood at Mass, water for baptizing, olive oil for all the "anointing" sacraments, and so on. The meaning of the sacraments can never change, nor can what the person—priest or otherwise—intends to do when he performs an act of liturgy. Lots of things *can* change, however, for example the words of the consecration at Mass, or the formula of baptism. Both of these must be based on what Christ said in the gospel, but the syntactical form has differed at various times in various rites. You may already know that the formula of consecration in the Roman Mass is not exactly the same as any of the four places in the New Testament that tell what our Lord said at the Last Supper.

A better example would be the formula used for absolution in the sacrament of penance, or that used for anointing the five senses in the last

anointing ("extreme unction"). Each is different
for Eastern and Western Catholics. Yet all Catholics have the same faith, and through their rites
Christ acts in the same way.

The God-made prayers of the liturgy are the
Scriptures. We say this even though it is a human
literature as well. The book of gospels, then all
the rest of the New and the Old Testaments
(but especially the psalms), are essential to all
Christian liturgical prayer. What man has done
is make up prayers *based on* the Scriptures. The
main one is that great central prayer in which
the offering of Christ to God is done sacramen-
tally in the Mass. It is called the *canon* ("rule,"
"standard") in the West, and the *anaphora*
(a-naf-o-ra, "offering") in the East.

Other examples of prayers made up by men
are the "prefaces" that introduce the canon, the
prayers of the whole assembly, whether in the
fore-Mass (collect), at the end of the preparation of the gifts (secret), or after people have
received the Eucharist (postcommunion). These
prayers are usually brief and to the point in the
Roman rite. So is the Kyrie, nowadays; but at
one time it was a long "litany," and litanies are a
very fine example of man-made prayers in the
liturgy. The Fathers of the Council, in their
constitution on the sacred liturgy of December
4, 1963, have decreed that in the full-scale revision of the Roman rite of the Mass, there
should be added "prayers for all the faithful"
after the homily.

The liturgical book called the "ritual" is filled

with beautiful man-made prayers and blessings: for bread, and cheese, for the well-being of a mother-to-be, and over every knd of object for human use.

Liturgy is poetry. Its refrain or theme is set in the Bible, the "Book of the Acts of God." However, it allows and even invites variations on its great themes. When you read in the papers that it will take about five years before we have at our disposal the liturgical changes indicated by the Council, that is what is meant. It is not the language change that will take all that time but the actual reformation of the rites themselves.

18
The Canon
of the Mass

WHAT is the liturgy? It is the prayer of Christ and His Church.

Who are its ministers? Bishops, priests, deacons, etc., and in the sacrament of marriage, the people themselves. In a broader sense, the priestly people baptized and confirmed in Christ who make up the Church are the ministers of the liturgy.

Why is it offered? To praise God and beg that the work of salvation may continue in us now.

You will recall that we spoke about the *gestures* and *actions* of those who participate in the liturgy; about the *Word of God* that is announced and explained to God's family; about the *song* that tells of our joy in the love of God about the *objects* or things that are signs of the sanctifying action of the living Christ.

Now we should like to turn to the central deed in all liturgy which is the eucharistic action of

Mass. Central to *it*, of course, is that portion which contains the great exchange of gifts. We give Christ to God and He gives Him back to us as our food for eternal life. This part of the Mass, we have said, is called the *canon* (in Western rites) or the *anaphora* (in Eastern rites).

Before the canon, there is that preparation of gifts that we somewhat inaccurately call the "offertory." It helps us to form the intention of offering. The *real* offertory is, of course, the *canon* itself. Remember that the word anaphora means offertory or "up-bearing." *After* the canon, there is the sacred banquet or communion. This is introduced by the traditional prayer of Christians preparing to eat Christ's body, the *Our Father*.

Before the preparation of the gifts we have the entrance rite and the "service of the Word," and after communion, we have a thanksgiving prayer (postcommunion) and the final blessing.

In order to understand the Mass we have to begin in the middle of it—with the canon. If we started at the beginning or at the end and worked our way forward or backward, we would lose our sense of what really is of most importance in this eucharistic prayer.

The canon begins with the greeting that is usual in liturgies: "The Lord be with you!" The people answer: "And with your spirit." Then comes the age-old suggestion: "All hearts heavenward." The answer comes: "They are directed to the Lord." Finally there is the invitation that pinpoints everything: "Let us offer a eucharist to the

Lord (*i.e.,* bless, praise, thank Him)," to which the people answer: "It is entirely fitting that we do so."

From this point until the concluding doxology, . . . ("through Him [Christ] and with Him and in Him all honor and glory is given to You, O God, Father Almighty, in the unity of the Holy Spirit, for ever and ever—Amen"), there is *one* prayer, and one only. At the heart of this prayer is the action of consecration. The whole canon makes holy our gift by our joining Christ (in sign) in His offering of Himself to the heavenly Father, and the Father's making this food sacred through its becoming the living flesh of His Son.

The canon is a single prayer. As a single prayer it effects the changing of bread and wine into the body and blood of Jesus, now in glory.

Over the centuries a number of prayers and invocations were added to the canon, making its basic unity hard to discover but not destroying it. One of the earliest of these additions was the *Sanctus* hymn. Then a number of phrases were added that spoke about "offering the gifts," and "having them ready"; other phrases that pray for the living and the dead; phrases in awe and gratitude for what has just happened.

But the main theme of the canon remains. It is a single great prayer of thanks (eucharist) to God for His mighty deeds of salvation, in the heart of which His greatest deed is recalled in sign: the death, resurrection, and ascension of His Son, to save us unto God's glory.

19

The Service
of the Word

WHEN we speak about the central part of the Mass, the canon or anaphora, we must take care. When we say that anything is "more" or "less" important in the Mass, we are speaking of a sacred action that is basically *one*. We should never think about the "principal parts" of the Mass in such a way that we try to see how late we can come or how early we can leave without missing anything.

There's a good reason for caution about the idea of principal parts. If the canon has a central place in the Mass—and it does—then, the action that prepares our minds and hearts for it is of key value also. This can likewise be said of the action that completes the Mass. Let's take a look at the preparatory action first.

God can speak to us in many ways and teach us in many ways. Creation "speaks" about its

Creator and "tells" us many things about God. In a sense, everything that happens in life is like a Word of God to us. The fact that we have to move to another town; the fact of getting sick; the fact of difficulties and troubles: God is speaking to us through all these events in our lives and He does want us to learn. The Word God speaks to us is personal through the speech of our work associates or the conversation of our family members or friends. God speaks with a thousand voices.

But He has spoken to us most clearly through Jesus, His only Son. This taking on of human nature by the eternal Word was, in a way, God's final Word to us. Never again will He speak so definitely, so fully, and so lovingly as in the Word incarnate.

If God's great act among us is His sharing of His life with us in His Son (His own Word), then it is Christ acting through the sacraments who continues to *speak* and *do* what His Father wills.

We can miss the message of God's Word and God's action, whether in nature, in our daily lives, or in the sacraments, if we are not alert and attentive to it. That is why the Church will never perform a sacred sign—a sacrament—without preparing us to take in its meaning. Her principle is this: no deed of God through Christ, no sacrament nor even a simple blessing, without first the action of the Holy Spirit through the reading of the Word of Scripture.

The Mass is that time in the life of the Christian when the living God speaks to us in a *special* way. We call those readings from the Bible in the early part of the Mass, the "service of the Word." Those holy pages are God's revelation of Himself. If the first reading happens to be from the book of Exodus or the book of Wisdom, Christ the incarnate Word is there—in promise. If it is a gospel reading, He is there as having come—in fulfillment. If it is an epistle of Saint Paul or Saint John or Saint Peter that is read, we are given the meaning of Christ's words—a further insight into the treasured words themselves. The *homily* or *sermon* is the concluding part of the service of the Word. It meditates on the living Word that has just been proclaimed. It is a real part of the liturgy, not just an optional appendage.

During October and November of 1962 and 1963 the Second Vatican Council considered this question: "How can God's Word in the liturgy be made to mean more to men?" We know the answers that the fathers of the Council have given for making the service of the Word meaningful.

The service of the Word is to be made more interesting through a greater variety of readings from Scripture at Mass; not the same epistle and gospel on the same Sunday every year, in other words. It will speak to us in one language only, our own. It will need to be spoken more forcefully (loudly, clearly, musically) than now; and it must be spoken more effectively through sermons that really mine the riches of the Bible. All these things the Council fathers have said.

The service of the Word is a *public* preparation for the eucharistic action that is at the heart of the Mass. But we should also read and study God's Word *privately* if we want the Holy Spirit to stir us when we listen at the service of the Word. If we prepare for Mass by reading over the Scripture texts beforehand our acting along with Christ in the Mass will be that much the more effective.

20
The Communion
of the Mass

THE Mass is a perfect sacrifice, that is, an offering to God. The Mass is the perfect self-offering of Jesus Christ to His heavenly Father. It is not Calvary "done again," but the one same offering done differently: this time not by Christ alone but by Christ and the Church, in sign.

If the gift of Christ to God is already perfect, it need not be repeated in sign unless something is going to result that would not happen otherwise. God is praised by men in the celebration of the liturgy. That much is sure. But we can not say too often that, while He doesn't need our praise, *we very much need to praise Him.* In other words, the benefit comes to *us* when we worship God in love.

Are we to say, then, that when the Church joins with the Lord Jesus in His obedient act of self-giving, her members are fulfilled, perfected, sanctified? Well, yes and no. *Yes,* in the sense that, unless the members of Christ unite themselves with Him in praise of God, little benefit can come to them. *No,* in the sense that, unless they *eat of the table* at which they have offered their gift, they may never undergo any change whatever.

The Mass is not chiefly a speaking over food by a priest (though it includes that). It is not just a raising up of the body and blood of the Lord for all to see. (As a matter of fact, this action was introduced more than a thousand years after Christ was glorified). *Before anything else, the Mass is an eating of sacred food.* The purpose of the eating—which is done in a spirit of charity—is to bring men closer to God in a way that no other human activity can bring them.

That is why we said in the previous chapter that there is a sense in which no part of the Mass liturgy is more important than any other. Unless the Scriptures are read, preached on, and thought about, neither priest nor people will be *prepared* for what is to follow. Unless the gifts of bread and wine are made ready, these gifts cannot become the Lord's body and blood. Without the consecration during the canon of the Mass (the change whereby Christ is offered to God), it would not be possible to eat the holy meal that is the source of God's life in us.

The Mass is one action. It is *completed* in the joyous union of God and man at the moment we receive His beloved Son as our bread of life. We call this union a "communion." Do you see the word "common" in "communion"?

(There is also a Latin word for "strengthen" hidden in there but that is a longer story). God and we have something in common. Christ is one with the Father because He has been raised up in glory as a reward for His obedience. In communion, we are made one with the Father through and in Christ. The meal we eat is the sign of an inner reality: our sharing in the divine life. It doesn't only signify it; it brings it about—makes us live. Do you begin to realize why we are told by Christ the Lord to "take and eat"?

It is possible to praise God through the Mass without "receiving communion"; possible for certain ones who offer it, anyway. But the Church will never permit Mass to be offered unless someone receives: at the very least the priest, and at best everyone who attends. You can see why. If no one ate the Lord's body, the Mass would then be a sacred change and a sacred offering, but it would not be a sacred meal. But if it were not a sacred meal, it could not be the Mass. The essential thing about the Mass, we repeat, is that *it is a meal.*

Why not try to make sure that whenever you are at Mass you not only *offer* but also *receive?* Make your participation in Mass perfect. A man who is a guest at someone's table and does not eat there must have a very good reason; otherwise his host will think him rude. Is he ill? Perhaps he did not know that the invitation included dinner. He will be a ghost at the feast until he joins the others in the very thing he and they were invited for.

21
The Fore-Mass
and Dismissal Rite

EVERYTHING that men do needs a beginning and an end. God saves us through rites that continue for a certain length of time. One thing follows another. At Sunday Mass our whole week is made prayerful and holy by what happens during the passage of this one hour.

The early portion of the Mass we call the fore-Mass. It is in two main parts, the entrance rite and the service of the Word. We have already spoken of the latter, which is made up of a first Scripture reading (though some celebrations like the ember days have more than one), commonly called the epistle, a second Scripture reading from one of the four gospel writers, and the homily or sermon on the Word of God that has just been proclaimed. Other parts of the service of the Word which we have not yet referred to are the responses that should be made by the choir or by all the people to the first reading (the gradual, the Alleluia verse, and the tract). These responses are always made up of verses of the Psalms, and are always joyous in tone (well, except for the prevailing gloom of the Masses for the dead, composed in the middle ages; but Vatican II has ordered that in their revision their paschal character should be restored—color of vestments and all).

In the Roman rite the only response provided for after the gospel is a quiet-voiced, "Praise be to you, O Christ." Many congregations, however, sing to the Lord Jesus an "acclamation" or pious outcry set to music, after the gospel reading. After this will come the newly decreed "common prayers" in which the people must partake—probably in litany form.

The final portion of the service of the Word is our proclamation of faith through the creed. The creed we say at Mass is basically that published at the Council of Nicaea in 325, drawn up against a priest named Arius who denied the full godly status of the Son of God. Some phrases were added to it later in the same century after another meeting of Catholic bishops from all over, at Constantinople in 381. Because of the numerous and complicated Latin phrases of the creed, many congregations have been making another choice. They recite or sing in English the Apostles' Creed, their own baptismal creed which they know so well. With full freedom of priests and people to pray in English, however, the Nicean Creed will be used as is proper.

The creed is the prayer with which the fore-Mass ends. How does it begin? With an entrance rite, a song in praise of God as the priest and servers enter the sanctuary. The chant provided in the missal is called the introit ("he enters") to describe what is going on. This, too, is normally taken from the book of Psalms or at least from the Bible. It is highly important to sing on this occasion, for that is what the introit is all about. As a poor substitute, the priest must recite the prayer, but that involves celebrating his own appearance on the scene—something like ringing the doorbell and then going in to receive yourself from the other side of the threshold!

The priest's private preparation for Mass, Psalm 42 and a confession of sinfulness, have "crept up" into the sanctuary over the years, just as his private departure prayer, the beautiful opening of Saint John's gospel, has done. Actually, the dismissal rite is a brief matter of the priest's saying, "Go, the Mass is over," followed by the solemn blessing. It is all but certain that in the revised Roman rite the Mass will close with this blessing, just as it will open with the entrance song.

22

Second Passion Sunday through the Great Sabbath Rest

WE HAVE been speaking of all sorts of things connected with the praise the whole Church gives to God through the liturgy, in Head and members. Symbols, Scripture, seasons; the structure of the ritual books and especially the structure of the great act of liturgy which is the Mass. But like everything else connected with religion, as soon as liturgy becomes complicated it threatens to lose its meaning.

The whole meaning of the liturgy is love and praise. These two ideas, basically one, are simplicity itself. The center of all liturgical action is the death and resurrection of the Lord Jesus. This is the one *mystery of faith* by which we are saved. All we really need to understand about the liturgy is that it brings into our life, through signs, the mystery of love which saves us.

God's love in Christ has three stages: it starts with Him who has loved us first, who creates us, and who sends His Son to bring us to Himself. This love of God is answered (stage two) by a love of the perfect Man, the God-man Jesus Christ, who loves the Father without any holding back. In stage three, God begins to love us for a new reason. He sees His Son imaged in us. All this, remember, takes place "in the Holy Spirit," that divine person who is all Love.

What we do when we pray as the Church is unite ourselves in love with the Jesus who died and rose to save us. Any sacrament, any sacramental or prayer offered to God by the Christian body, is a means to make available to us the death and resurrection of Christ which fills us with the Father's love.

That is why there is nothing so important in the Christian year as "paschaltide." In the New Testament, Christ's "pasch" means all His sufferings and all His glorification, not simply His being raised up from the dead. It means His passage from death to life, from the desert of suffering to the promised land of glory, from the Egyptian darkness of sin to the bright light of the Father's kingdom. Christ's pasch means *for us* our passage from sin to grace; from having to die to an immortal life in the body with the Father.

The whole action is commemorated in the

"Great Night of Easter," that vigil which ends in the Mass of the Resurrection. Ever since Bishop Cyril's time in Jerusalem (starting in 348 or 349 A.D.), the one mystery of Christ has been acted out over a week's time, just as in real life. At the close of Lent there comes the First Sunday of Passiontide, two weeks before Easter. A procession with palms is held on what we now call the Second Sunday of Passiontide. The first three days of the week ("Holy Week") are uneventful. On Sunday our Lord's trial and sufferings are read from Saint Matthew's gospel; then on Tuesday and Wednesday comes the reading of Mark's and Luke's accounts. We will read John's report of the passion at the Communion Service of Good Friday.

On Thursday we recall Jesus' gift of the Eucharist to us at the last supper. There are only two Masses prescribed for Holy Thursday: one is the Mass of the Holy Oils offered by the bishop in the cathedral church in the morning; the other is the *one* Mass celebrated in each church at night to symbolize by its very *one*ness the fact that the Eucharist is the sacrament of unity. The new conciliar constitution of the liturgy says that at each of these the priests should "concelebrate," *i.e.*, all offer the same Mass to manifest the unity of the priesthood and of the sacrifice that the Mass is.

There is no Mass offered on Friday. Christ's eucharistic body is placed in a specially made shrine for our veneration. There we praise God who leaves our great Intercessor among us over the ages in this sign. Then He is "taken away" on Friday (to be eaten, actually, in the Communion Service). In this way we act out the Lord's absence from us in death. A carved image of Christ on the cross takes the place of the true image of Christ which is the Eucharist; we pay honor to this crucifix. With the Lord gone from our altar and our tabernacle we try to recapture the spirit of the earth's desolation during the hours He lay in the tomb.

It is a calm period, a time of thirty hours or so, in which we have the chance to turn over in our minds the sobering thought that the stillness of death has overtaken the world's Savior. A "paschal fast" marks the entire two days. They are only a prelude, though. We are getting ready to celebrate the bursting of the rock tomb by Him whom neither death nor grave could hold. We are about to shout with joy, "Alleluia! He is risen!"

23
The Paschal Vigil and Easter Mass

"WHY is this night different from all other nights of the year?" This is the question asked at the Jewish Passover meal by the youngest family member of the eldest from ancient times, *i.e.*, the day of Moses. It was a question put by one of Jesus' fishermen friends at the last supper to Him whom they revered as "Rabbi," their teacher.

The solemn answer that had to be given ran thus: "This night is different because we celebrate the most important moment in the history of our people. On this night we celebrate their going forth in triumph from slavery to freedom."

The Christian liturgy is built on the Hebrew liturgy. Of old, the people of God looked back to their release from Egyptian slavery described in the book of Exodus (10:2; 12:26; 13:8). They also looked forward to a new Passover to come, a complete and final fulfillment of all

79

their hopes for freedom, happiness, and peace.

Christians have the same memories as Israel; they are one people with them. Therefore they, too, look back on the night they fled from Pharaoh, but only because it foreshadowed a much greater night different from all others: the night when Christ passed from the darkness of the tomb to the light of risen life.

Like the Jews of Jesus' day, Christians also look ahead. They look to a fulfillment that is both complete in itself and complete *in them*—to the Last Day, when Christ our Light shall appear.

This is what we Christians celebrate on the vigil of Easter and in the Easter Mass.

It is the center of all Christian liturgy because it celebrates the deed of God which is at the center of human life. Christ's death and resurrection become part of our lives in every Mass, in every act of liturgy. This is especially true, however, when in word and gesture and song we recall the saving deed itself, in all its detail.

First there is the rite of fire—a spark struck from steel on a flinty rock—because this is the night of the New Light. Then a candle is blessed: Christ the pillar of fire who goes before His people in the darkened church as did the Lord God in the desert journey. "May the light of Christ in glory, rising again," we pray, "dispel the darkness of heart and mind." Forward goes the Lord Jesus, in the symbol of the Easter candle. Three times we cry out our thanks to God for this "Light of Christ."

We mount the candle in the sanctuary, incense

it, then sing the praises of the Father who has saved us. The candle is not merely a tall cylinder of wax, it is *Christ with us.*

Then we bless the baptismal waters, piercing them from time to time with the Christ-candle, blessing them with the breath of the Spirit.

The Scriptures are read next: the creation story from Genesis, the deliverance story from Exodus, Isaia telling of the cleansing of the Temple, and Moses (in Deuteronomy) praising the words of God's holy Law. In response a litany is sung—phrase following phrase like the rolling of waves on the beach.

What God promised His people Israel in the Scriptures He fulfills in the saints of the new Law, the men and women who live by the gospel: "Peter . . . Paul . . . Benedict . . . Dominic . . . Francis . . . Agnes . . . Cecilia . . . pray for us." Embedded deep in the litany is a reminder of that drowning that made new men—saints—of us. We repeat after the priest our baptismal promises. Christ rises from the dead, comes up from the Red Sea of His drenching in pain; but He does not rise alone; we rise with Him.

We go forward then, to celebrate the paschal Eucharist—to eat the manna that gives life and drink the water struck from the rock: the bread and wine that is the Lord.

There is no liturgy in all the year like that of the Great Night of Easter. It ends in a new day. But it does not really *end* there. The celebration looks forward to the new Day that is yet to come —the Day that is never-ending.

24 ✗

Liturgical Movement: What Does It Mean?

A "MOVEMENT" of any kind means activity in a direction. Things "get moving" because they've been inactive, quiet, undisturbed. It cannot for a moment be said of the liturgy that Christ the Lord has not been active to save us through it by means of holy signs and through the Scriptures; for of course He has. That is what liturgy is: the Church's work of praise in which Christ is active.

We of the Church, however, have not always known clearly how He was working to save us. We have fallen into stodgy ways of speaking about the mystery of Christ (His death and resurrection which give life to believers). We have used human speech to describe the truth of what we believe when the words of the Holy Spirit say it much better.

We have forgotten the symbolism of gesture

and movement—all that goes to make up the particular "ritual" of a sacrament or sacramental, or an entire "rite." We can no longer speak or understand the languages in which we pray. We don't fully realize the connection between a sign of love and the love (or "grace") that it brings us. That in good part is because the sign is so hard to find, or sometimes even to *see*.

In brief, the activity of our Lord, gloriously reigning with His Father, has been *hidden* in the liturgy when the whole purpose of liturgy is to *disclose* His activity, make it clear to us. The mysteriousness of His action in the Church doesn't grow less as the liturgy makes it evident to us. We see Christ's deed as even more mystery-laden because we see it more clearly in word and sign.

The liturgical movement, therefore, is the activity of all in the Church—bishops, priests, and people—as they look deeply into the action of Christ worshiping His Father, then do the same thing on earth under His headship.

Movement means *progress* if it's well thought-out movement. The liturgical movement is progress for the whole Church in the direction of the heavenly sanctuary. We are all going forward together to the resurrected life in this body, where we will forever praise the Father and Christ the Lamb in the Holy Spirit.

The best sign of this forward movement is the praise we offer God in our earthly sanctuaries in the Eucharist. But of course this formal sacramental praise is the sign of the love of neighbor we show in a thousand ways: fighting segregation, getting decent housing and a fair wage for all, treating everyone we meet as a *brother* and not just as another unit or object.

Actually there is something more to the liturgical movement than what we have just described. Above we spoke of worship, and the chief overflow of worship which is charity, as if *they* were the liturgical movement. What they are is the Church's liturgical life, and that of course is the great matter. The "movement" in a strict sense is the rediscovery and the expression of that life. Over the last forty years (or seventy or eighty, if you start down at the roots) scholars have been studying the Fathers of the Church and the Church's early liturgies and the deeper meanings of the Bible. Through knowing exactly where she has been, they have discovered the direction in which the Church should be going.

Scholars don't really "get the Church moving again," however. That is for bishops to do, with the fruits of other men's studies giving them the lead.

That is why we say that in the liturgical movement the bishops must lead their people in sacramental celebration or *there is no movement*.

The bishops at Vatican II by a vote of 2,147 to 4, on December 4, 1963, got the Church "moving again" in the all-important matter of bringing the saving work of God in Christ into the lives of men!

25
The Liturgy and the Care of Souls

ONE of the most important things that happened at the Second Council of the Vatican was the opening talk of Pope John XXIII. The fathers of the council didn't go to Rome to "rubber stamp" decisions that the Holy Father had already made. That isn't the way a council works. Popes John and Paul are members of the council along with their brother bishops. Still the Pope is clearly its leading figure. When he makes suggestions or proposals, the others listen with special attention.

Among other things, Pope John said in this first talk: "The substance [the content] of the ancient teaching of the deposit of faith [what we believe, having been taught it by Christ and the apostles] is one thing; the way in which it is presented is another. The latter fact must be taken into account—if necessary, in a spirit of great patience. Everything must be viewed in the light of a teaching responsibility that is *predominantly pastoral.*"

He meant, of course, that while he and his brother bishops can never change the belief of the Church, they must constantly be making changes so that the flock of Christ—His sheep, we ourselves—will understand the holy teaching that will bring us salvation.

There are some in the Church who will always have trouble understanding change. They want things to stay just as they knew them when they were boys. But the Pope says that the pastoral office must come first; in other words, the Church must worry about the needs of her members and not about keeping things the way "they always were" for sentimental reasons.

This outlook of Pope John was supported very strongly by the bishops at the Council when they voted on Dec. 7, 1962, on the first chapter of what came to be a constitution in seven chapters, "General Principles for Renewing and Promoting the Sacred Liturgy." The vote was 1,922 for, and 11 against, the proposed changes (there were another 180 in favor, but with some ideas of their own). One of the early achievements of these changes is that the people will be able to hear God's Word addressed to them in their own language. This may be happening in your part of the world by the time you read this. People are singing out joyfully in response to God's Word again in their own tongue. The dialogue they carry on with the bishop or priest who celebrates will mean much more to them then, because they are using the only language most of them know.

Much more important, it will become clear as a result of changes in the liturgy of the Mass exactly what we are doing in union with Christ, while we are doing it. As things stand now, people need big, fat missals—or explanations like those attempted in this book—to tell them what's going on. Simply coming to Mass hasn't been doing the job—as any non-Catholic guest at our liturgy or any thoughtful Catholic will tell you.

It is supremely important, the bishops said in the document they voted on so strongly, that the exercise of Christ's priesthood by means of outward signs should be realized within the Church. Does this happen in fact? Can a person who doesn't read (or even one who can) come to Mass and learn there, from all he hears and does and sings and says, that by Christ's death and resurrection he is saved?

The answer to that question is "No." It has been "No" in the Western Church for almost fifteen hundred years now. The Pope and the bishops have said in General Council that all this has to change because of the pastoral needs of the Church. The hungry sheep look up, they say, and must be fed.

26
The Liturgy
and Catechism

LEARNING about one's religion is something
that normally takes place in the Catholic
school, the "school of religion," or the Confraternity of Christian Doctrine class. An additional
book like this one helps you to grow in faith
as an adult.

Sunday Mass in the parish church or in con-
junction with school life generally hasn't been
much of an occasion for making strides in our
knowledge of God. It *should* be, of course. It
just isn't. Because we don't celebrate the mysteries of our redemption very well we don't grow
in a knowledge of all that God has done for us—
is doing for us here and now—at this Mass, in
this reception of penance, at this baptism, or
wedding, or funeral. We learn most of what we
know about God's life in us outside of and apart
from the times when we are *receiving* it!

The whole thing is topsy-turvy, of course. The earliest way the Church had of sharing the Christ-life with her children—for centuries the only way—was the sacramental celebration of the "mystery of Christ." There were no schools, no Confraternity classes, no catechisms, no Paulist paperbacks. People became Catholics and very good ones, all because they were led into the reality of being alive in Christ simply through *doing* it; not by reciting questions and answers about it, not by reading columns on the subject, nor having inquiry classes or study clubs on liturgical participation.

Take the matter of having one book about liturgy, another on the moral life of Christians, and still another on the unity of the Church. A Christian who lived in the year 400 wouldn't know what to make of that. He'd say, "What's got into you? You've divided everything up. Forming people in Christ is all the one thing, isn't it? It happens chiefly through the liturgy doesn't it? Please take back your booklets (which I find interesting) and your catechisms (which I find dull), and lead me to the nearest parish church!"

We'd have to make all sorts of excuses after that. We'd need to explain what *had* got into us these last fifteen or sixteen centuries. But we could say one clear thing, at least. We could point out that we're in the midst of a great meeting of all our bishops—the twenty-first ecumenical council—in which we are trying to put the Humpty-Dumpty of catechizing and sacramental celebration and moral life back together again.

It's as simple as this: the great sacrament (or sign) of all that God has done for us is Jesus Christ. Our Lord's death on the cross and His glorification are what give us life. Right now, Jesus is back in glory at His Father's right hand. The great sacrament (or sign) of Jesus that is present to us is the Church. It still lives. We are in it, of it; it surrounds us. To have the Spirit dwell in us is to be alive in the Church and to be alive in Christ. The lesser signs of these two great signs, Christ and the Church, are the well-known seven sacraments, of which the Eucharist and holy baptism are the chief.

You and I are going to see all sorts of wonderful things come out of the Second Vatican Council. High on the list is a Church-wide realization of who Jesus Christ is as our great priest; how He saves us through His death and resurrection; how *His* risen life becomes *our* life every time any portion of the liturgy—but chiefly the Mass liturgy—is celebrated by us under His headship.

Does this mean that all catechisms, and catechism classes, and books like this one will run a poor second to taking our proper part in the liturgy? Let's hope so. Why? *Because there is no fit substitute for first having God's living Word proclaimed to us, and then going forward immediately to celebrate in the Church those signs of Christ that give life.*

27
Progress
in the Liturgy

THERE has been great progress made in celebrating the mystery of Christ *in sacrament* over the last one hundred years. In Europe some early great names in the restoration of the treasure of public worship to the Church were those of Benedictine monks. Germany, for example, was led by two brothers named Placidus and Maurus Wolter, of the Abbey of Beuron.

At Solesmes (So-lem) in France the great figure was Dom Prosper Gueranger. Coming down to our own day (for those men lived a hundred years ago), two persons to whom we owe a great debt are Dom Ildefons Herwegen (Hare-vay-ghen), Abbot of Maria Laach in Germany, and Dom Lambert Beauduin of Mont-Cesar Abbey in Louvain, Belgium.

The only trouble with celebrating Christ as monks do is that life in a monastery isn't very much like life in a parish. And most Christian

men and women live in this or that parish, in
such and such a city or town. They are insurance
men, farmers, factory workers, housewives. They
do not rise at four-thirty each morning; they do
not know Latin as a second language; they do
not know how to sing the divine office.

For all these reasons liturgical prayer in monasteries—no matter how beautifully it is carried
out—is not a pattern which parish churches can
follow. Yet Pope Pius XI reminded us in the
letter he wrote establishing the Feast of Christ
the King that no official teaching of the Church
concerning doctrine is nearly so effective in people's lives as the celebration of the Christian Sunday and the annual cycle of feasts.

That is why the progress in scholarship and
study about the liturgy in the monasteries, and
about sacred art, sacred music and church architecture, had to make its way outside monastic
walls and into the everyday life of the Church.
People in the parishes had to recite and sing, and
walk in procession, and hear God's Word proclaimed to them in a clear tone if they were
really to understand the meaning of baptism,
or the Eucharist, or marriage, or Christian burial.

They needed, in other words, to take part
actively in the work of praise being done by
Christ through the leadership of His priests: that
means they had to understand its meaning first,
in order to be made holy by it. Now the chief
"activity" of the man who prays takes place in
deep corners of his heart. In that sense, it has
always been possible to "participate actively" in

the liturgy, even when all a person understood about it was that "God's body" was being held up by the priest at Mass to be adored. That isn't knowing very much about the Mass, or even anything very clear or very central about it.

In a time like our own, this small fragment of knowledge isn't of much use when the job that needs to be done is joining Christ actively in the worship of His Father. For that, all the prayers and all the Scripture readings and all the symbols and gestures of the Mass need to be given meaning for us. Otherwise we'll just go through the motions all our lives and never take a deep part in celebrating "the mystery of faith."

In the '20s and the '30s millions of people began to use missals at Mass. That was progress in the liturgy. Thousands of school children and adults came to learn something about Gregorian chant. That, too, was progress.

It could all have come to nothing, though. In fact, it almost did come to nothing. But in 1955, Pope Pius XII reformed the Holy Week and Easter liturgy in the Western Church. From that date down to December 4, 1963 (the great affirmative vote of the bishops on the liturgy in Vatican Council II and its promulgation by Pope Paul VI), there has been nothing but progress in the prayer life of the Western Church.

There is still a long way to go. It will take lifetime upon lifetime of prayer and hard work before the whole Church becomes a single choir on earth giving praise to the Blessed One, in the Spirit, through Christ the Lamb.

28
The Church Reforms
Her Liturgy

THERE are some things in life that cannot be reformed, but they are not very many. Nature and its laws, for example, are fixed. They can be discovered; they can be acted on, and put to good use; but they cannot be changed.

God's living Word cannot be changed, either. That means that the mystery of faith, which is the way God saves us in Christ, is not to be reformed or refashioned by men. Christ reigns in heaven forevermore. He brings us to life in Himself—through the action of the Holy Spirit— in the power of the gospel and those saving signs we call the sacraments. We do not change this order of things. We learn it and, coming to know it, we love it. We do not reform it.

What the Church constantly does is change *her* ways of doing things (not *God's* ways), to meet the needs of her many children. When the Christians in Rome stopped speaking Greek she changed the Mass into Latin, the living language of the Roman people. She had already worked out one form of celebration of the Eucharist in Jerusalem, another in northern Egypt, and still another in Antioch in Syria because the people differed in their customs and outlook in those three places.

Then something happened to change all this. The gospel was spread to new nations, to wild tribes, to people whose tongues the missionaries did not know. Many of these languages—those of the barbarians of northern Europe and Asia, for example—were not written down anywhere. Therefore the Bible stayed in Latin and Greek, and so did the service books of the liturgy like the Missal and the Ritual and Pontifical (containing the other sacraments). This time the Church did not adapt herself because she could not. She felt the task was too big for her. The sole exception to this was in the conversion of the Slavs, where Saints Cyril and Methodius gave the people their own liturgy in their own customs and language. The missionary thrust out of Rome and out of the Irish monasteries felt unequal to this task.

Even though there were lots of "reforms" accomplished at the time of the Council of Trent, the liturgical reforms were only of minor matters like the editing of the Latin Missal and the Office. *Basic* liturgical reforms did not take place. The gospel of Christ continued to be brought to far-off places like Africa, China and the Americas in a fundamentally European (indeed Roman) way. The result? Many came to faith, but only with difficulty. Many others—millions of people—never came to faith.

The Church has been engaged in certain reforms in her liturgy over the last fifty years. Chiefly, she has been allowing all sorts of exceptions where the bishops of whole countries ask for them. "May we baptize, may we marry, may we bury our people in such and such a way?" "May we read these and these parts of the Mass in the people's own language?" "May we stop this particular custom in the liturgy? It is meaningless—or offensive—to our people." To all this the Holy See has been saying "Yes."

That kind of thing is called relaxing the law. It is not really liturgical reform. The greatest single reform we have had of our Roman liturgy in the last four hundred years, as we have mentioned, came in 1955. A new rite of Holy Week, and especially the three sacred days at the end, was given to the West. It is a nearly perfect rite in its structure, with the possible exception of the Scripture readings in the Easter vigil service. Everything else about it is understandable, or can readily be made so, except for the language.

The bishops of the Church and other "Fathers" at Vatican Council II have voted resoundingly in favor of certain general principles and specific changes that will govern the imminent, genuine liturgical reform. The readers of these lines will see in their lifetimes changes in Catholic worship such as have not been made in thirteen or fourteen centuries (longer in the East).

Isn't that a little frightening?

There is something even more frightening. It is the idea of not having brought Christ to men and men to Christ because we did not have the faith or the courage for long centuries to make reforms in our liturgy.

29

Rites and Languages
in Liturgy

O N A basketball court, the players are active
at all times between any two blasts of the
referee's whistle. Their movements are much the
same whether the game is played in the baking
sun of Saudi Arabia or in a packed gym in south-
ern Indiana. Why? Because it has been found
that if the rules of the game are followed, a certain set of movements is best suited to get the
ball up the court and into the basket.

The actions of all glass blowers everywhere are
the same, except for the matter of equipment; of
lathe operators; of hairdressers. In each of these
cases, the movement or behavior of the worker
is determined by the task he has set himself to
accomplish.

Quite different from this, however, is the way
people in different parts of the world enter and
leave a room in the presence of their superiors.

The signs of affection and friendship, such as kissing and shaking hands, are not the same everywhere. Some people wear white to mourn the dead, some black; many kneel to pray, some never kneel; and so on.

There are differences, then, between *functional* behavior (getting the job done), and *conventional* behavior (agreed-upon patterns of carrying out a certain activity). The question for us is: what kind of behavior goes to make up a sacred rite? If you wish to move a missal or drink from a cup, isn't there only one way of doing it, pretty much? Yet the Church has numerous rites, both in the broader sense of the Roman rite, the Byzantine rite, etc., and in the narrower sense of the offertory rite, the communion rite, within each one of those above. Are the rites and languages used in the worship of God a practical matter, or are they a matter of custom, or are they both?

The question almost answers itself in the matter of human speech. Language is for communication. It is the means by which God speaks His holy Word to us in inspired Scripture. By it, too, the Church speaks to our hearts so that we may pray better as her children. The language of liturgy, therefore, will either be immediately understood by both speaker and hearer (as with Catholics who pray the Mass in Arabic or English or Hindi), or it will need to be made intelligible by means of a missal or a person reading a translation (as at the present writing with Catholics who pray the Mass in Latin).

There is such a thing as feeling very much a
home on hearing the familiar sounds of a lan
guage one has never understood. Many Wester
rite Catholics have this feeling. They neve
could follow the epistle in Latin in their hom
parish in Olyphant, Pennsylvania, and they un
derstand it no better in Santa Rosa, California
or Paris, but there it reminds them of Catholi
life as they know it in Olyphant. We call tha
"the virtue of the familiar."

This kind of familiarity is a virtue, but be
coming familiar with exactly what God is sayin
to us as He says it, and what we are saying t
Him in response, is an even greater virtue. It is
in fact, the very virtue (i.e. the power or pur
pose) of language.

The general principle is that—though a sacre
tongue may be archaic and used in liturgy only
(as Church Slavonic is to many modern Slavi
peoples), it must convey ideas to us, not just pro
vide feelings as music and incense and a familia
mumble do.

When it comes to rites it is much the same
When Chinese Christians pray the liturgy thei
bodily movements and indeed their whole rit
must say "sacred," "holy," to them *as Chinese
It is no good to say: "But everyone in fourth-cen
tury Constantinople—or sixth-century Rome—
was agreed that this is the way to prepare the
gifts of bread and wine, or to give the kiss o
peace." The Chinese Catholic will rightly say,
"I am a man of twentieth-century Taipei and i
is foreign to me. My people have been praying

for thousands of years. Please let us pray to God through Christ in *our* way."

For us in the West, slow, stately movement conveys an idea of the eternal God. For us kneeling is a posture of prayer. Standing erect is an even more significant one, and even more universally employed. To walk in procession, at times carrying a sacred object, has meaning for us. So does the exercise of sight and scent and sound.

Whenever a Catholic speaks of reforms in the liturgy, therefore, whether of language or rite or both, what he is talking about is framing the most important action a man can do in life in terms of the speech and movement that are already second nature to him.

As you might expect, the Fathers of the Vatican Council voted to revise thoroughly *all* the sacred rites of the Western Church, lest they grow meaningless and thus fail of their very purpose.

30
Sacred Art and Liturgy

THERE's an old proverb that says, "Art consists in veiling art." That means that the more a poem (or picture or statue) shouts at you, "See what a poem (or picture or statue) am I!" the less deserving it is of our attention. Real art, in other words, makes its point by simply *being* what it is. The viewer—or reader or hearer—puts himself in its presence and knows that he is the richer for it. He is improved in his whole being. He has a deeper inkling of the great beauty, harmony, and unity that is God.

This is what should happen to the Christian when he goes to his parish church or to any sacred place. He should experience something of the glory of God through the world of the senses. For this reason the Church has always been friendly to the arts: architecture, vestment-making, sculpture, organ music, and so on. She wants her children to come in touch with Him who is invisible through the splendor of things visible. This is, of course, the very principle used by God Himself in sending His Son to earth in human flesh. The Word of life was made visible, St. John says: the eternal life which dwelt with the Father we have seen and heard and bear testimony to (cf. I John 1:1-4). Our sacred art is likewise a testimony we Christians give to the Word of life which the Holy Spirit speaks in our hearts. Often, unfortunately, we cannot express this testimony very clearly because we do not hear His voice.

Some sad things have happened over the years with respect to art and the Catholic Church. There are whole cities and dioceses in this country, for example, that do not have a single church that is a true work of art; neither is there a fine art object to be found in even one of them. How can it be, one wonders, that while most of the major U.S. cities have first-class architects, craftsmen in metal, mosaic-tile, and stone, not one is ever asked to give glory to God with his gift? An even greater puzzle is how third- and fourth-rate professional men ("hucksters" really, when it comes to cracker-box Colonial churches, to plaster statuary and simpering wood) get hundreds of thousands of dollars worth of contracts. Where do the Catholic people get such a talent for cheating themselves by contracting for these ugly expressions of religious faith? If their faith in Jesus Christ is true, why is their art so false? There are no easy answers to these questions.

It has taken us hundreds of years to get into the
fix we're in. No quick inquiry into the problem
will account for it, much less a quick solution
take care of it. One thing fairly clear is that if
the arts were held in higher honor in seminaries
where future priests study, things would grow
better almost immediately. Then, too, if the
motherhouses where religious brothers and sisters
are formed were to be purged of bad hymns,
badly written religious books (for of course literature is a form of art), and bad furnishings in
chapel, the impact on Catholic life would soon be
evident. A third important area is that of the
schools the Church conducts. Even though less
than half of all Catholic children attend them,
these schools could help the whole body of the
Church immensely by good art education.

Are these matters so important, you may be
asking? Isn't true religion something that's in the
heart, not in hymns or baptisteries or colored
glass?

These things are terribly important. God has
so made us that nothing can take place in our
hearts (that is to say, our whole selves) except
through what we see and hear and *feel*. And we
are not likely to have an experience of God or of
Christ unless we sing and dance and play in our
worship once again, in temples that remind us of
the heavenly Jerusalem.

Slowly, through much anguish, the Western
Church is coming to know again what the East
has never forgotten, that there is no Christian
worship without song. This ancient truth is not

immediately acceptable to many—and for readily understood reasons. They were raised to think of contemplation in silence as the highest good of the Mass; of hymn-singing, which they normally did badly, as retrogression.

Don't get discouraged, you readers of this book who know what beauty is and who want to put it in the service of faith. Catholic priests and people are constantly becoming more aware of why only the best will do for the worship of Him who is the Holy.

is the Holy

31
The Liturgy
and Architecture

THE shape and structure of a building is determined by what goes on inside it. That, at least,
is the way things ought to be. Every building
shelters men against the weather, regardless of its
other purposes. In the case of a church, the basic
function of the building is to protect men against
sun and wind and rain while they worship their
heavenly Father through Jesus Christ in the Holy
Spirit.

There is more to a church than shelter, though.
Its lines should be governed by the sacred action
that takes place there. The altar is clearly the
central object or thing in a church. The area
where it stands, the sanctuary, should be spacious
enough that the movements of the priest and the
other ministers of the Mass (e.g., deacon and
subdeacon, servers, commentator, reader) can
take place easily within it. The altar should be

clearly seen as a *table*—since what takes place
at it is a sacrifice-meal—but above all it should
be *clearly seen*. The visibility of the priest's movements is of great importance. As we've tried to
point out before, his gestures tell what is happening at the altar as much as his words do. But if
his activity over the gifts of bread and wine can't
be seen, and his words can't be heard (or being
heard can't be understood), then the very sign
language which is the central feature of sacraments won't speak to the viewers and hearers.

Catholics at Mass should be more than viewers
and hearers, of course. They should be standers
and kneelers and movers-about in procession.
That means that the pews should be comfortable
(*space*, please, not foam rubber!), the aisles wide,
and places like the baptistery, the communion-
rail or communion-station area, and the vestibule,
roomy and ample.

If the altar is central to the eucharistic action
of the Mass, the pulpit and lectern or reading
desk need to stand out as distinct, for the proper
celebration of the service of the Word takes place
there. That means that there will be a kind of
crossing of two invisible lines for the human eye
to take in. One line runs between the worshiper
and the altar. The other one crosses in front of
the altar, from the point where the commentator
explains and reads to that point where the holy
gospel is proclaimed and the Scriptures are explained.

Do any of you who happen to be reading these
lines hope to be architects some day? Builders?

Construction engineers? Are some of you in that work now? If you are, or hope to be, you need to pray a lot and pray well in Masses in which you participate fully.

Then and only then will you know how to build a holy temple of God, because you will know—as so many church-builders of the past have not known—what a church is really for.

32
The Work of the Liturgical Conference

THE best way to keep a cause alive is for the people who love it most to band together and work to spread it in men's hearts. That is what happened in the case of Christianity, which is the love that *persons*, human and divine, have for one another. That is what happens in the growth of any important cause. There must be a banding together so that there may be a spreading.

Back in 1940 the Catholics in this country who had learned from their European brothers about the renewal of Christ's mystery in sacramental sign banded together to share their treasure. They formed the Liturgical Conference.

Before that time there had been a group of Benedictine monks who were extremely interested in the celebration of the liturgy as the chief means of grace in the Church. They included Father Virgil Michel (God grant him eternal rest), Father Michael Ducey (still very active), and the then Abbot Alcuin Deutsch of Saint John's Abbey, Collegeville, Minnesota. These men—and there were many others—decided that what had been developing through prayer and scholarly study in their monasteries needed to be shared with all the people of God.

The first meeting of what is now the national Liturgical Conference was held in downtown Chicago at the Cathedral Church of the Holy Name. Surely this was a proper setting for a movement that hoped to bring Christ into people's lives precisely where they lived and worked.

Last summer in Philadelphia at the twenty-fourth such annual meeting there were many more parishioners than there were priests or religious sisters and brothers—nearly 14,000 persons in all. This is just as it should be. Liturgical celebration is not a matter for the few, but for all who bear the name of *Christian*.

Also, it should be mentioned, the number of Protestant Christians who attend these "weeks" is ever on the increase. This is because the faith and piety of the Church are seen to be basically biblical in the liturgy—not a hodgepodge of little unrelated devotions and big unrelated doctrines.

There are by now several thousand members of the Liturgical Conference ranging from cardinal archbishops to busy homemakers. Anyone who has an interest in the celebration of the mystery of Christ in His Church may belong. The national office is at 3428 9th St., N.E., Washington, D. C. (20017).

This Conference has a general meeting in late August each year, but its much more important task is to help bishops and priests and people in parishes, and educators, celebrate the sacraments meaningfully. This is, one may say, the *central* area of the Conference's concern.

Hospitals are important in the life of the Church. So are the relief of the poor, and schools, and retreats, and the building of buildings. None of this matters, however—*it doesn't really matter at all*—unless everyone in the Church is quite clear on what it means to worship God in Jesus Christ.

Christians who have a knowing concern for the progress of the liturgy realize what Christianity is, however, and what it's for. If they don't love with a great love, that is doubly regrettable. But at least they have the meaning of the mystery straight.

They have seen a vision. It is the vision of the eternal pleading of Christ for us, at His Father's right hand, made real in time through the "sacrament" of God's Word and the "sacrament" of God's Deed, both made visible in sign.

Such is the vision that all Christians must have of their holy faith if indeed it is to be the authentic faith of the Church. To be concerned with liturgical worship is to be a man of the center, a person who does not waste his energies on secondary questions out at the edges of the mystery of Christ. A liturgical enthusiast is a balanced Christian.

Selected Reading

(All available in paper except Reinhold)

Baum, Gregory, O.S.A. *Word and Sacrament in the Church*. Glen Rock, N.J.: Paulist Press, 1963. 21 p.

Constitution on the Sacred Liturgy of the Second Vatican Council and the Motu Proprio of Pope Paul VI, with a commentary by Gerard S. Sloyan. Glen Rock, N.J.: Paulist Press, 1964. 86p.

Gallen, John, S.J. *Scripture Services*. Collegeville, Minn.: Liturgical Press, 1963. 160 p.

Howell, Clifford, S.J. *Preparing for Easter*. Collegeville, Minn.: Liturgical Press, 1957. 160p.

Jungmann, Joseph A., S.J. *The Sacrifice of the Church. The Meaning of the Mass*. Tr. Clifford Howell, S.J. Collegeville, Minn.: Liturgical Press, 1956. 71 p.

Klauser, Theodor. *A Brief History of Liturgy*. Collegeville, Minn.: Liturgical Press, 1953. 33p.

McManus, Frederick R. and Diekmann, Godfrey L. "A Commentary on the Constitution on Sacred Liturgy," *Worship*, 38 (May and June), 1964

Miller, John H., C.S.C. *Signs of Transformation in Christ*. Englewood Cliffs, N.J.: Prentice-Hall, 1963. 117p.

O'Shea, William, S.S. *The Meaning of Holy Week*. Collegeville, Minn.: Liturgical Press, 1958. 136p.

"Parish Worship Program," including a manual for priests, sermon outlines, a pamphlet for the laity, commentator's kit, etc. Washington: The Liturgical Conference, 3428 9th St. N.E., 20017, 1964.

Parsch, Pius. *Study the Mass*. Collegeville, Minn.: Liturgical Press, rev. ed. 1963. 128p.

Reinhold, H.A. *Bringing the Mass to the People*. Baltimore: Helicon, 1960. 114 p.

Tavard, George H., A. A. *Theology of the Word*. Glen Rock, N.J.: Paulist Press, 1963. 31p.

Some Other Western Liturgies

The Eucharistic Liturgy of Taizé. London: Faith Press, 1962. (Protestant).

Service for the Lord's Day and Lectionary for the Christian Year. Philadelphia: Westminster Press, 1964 (Protestant). 31-100-